This Journal Belongs To:

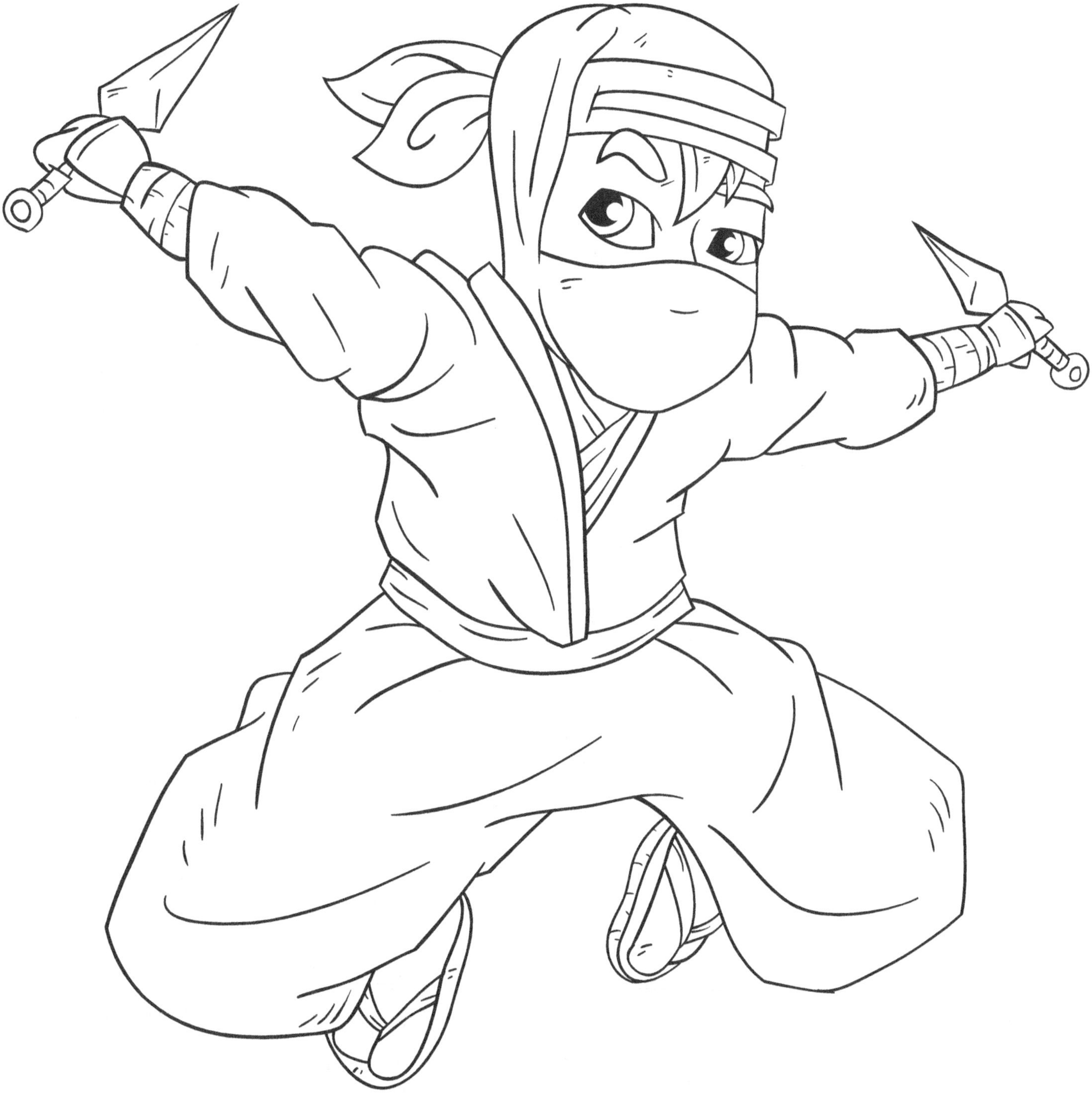

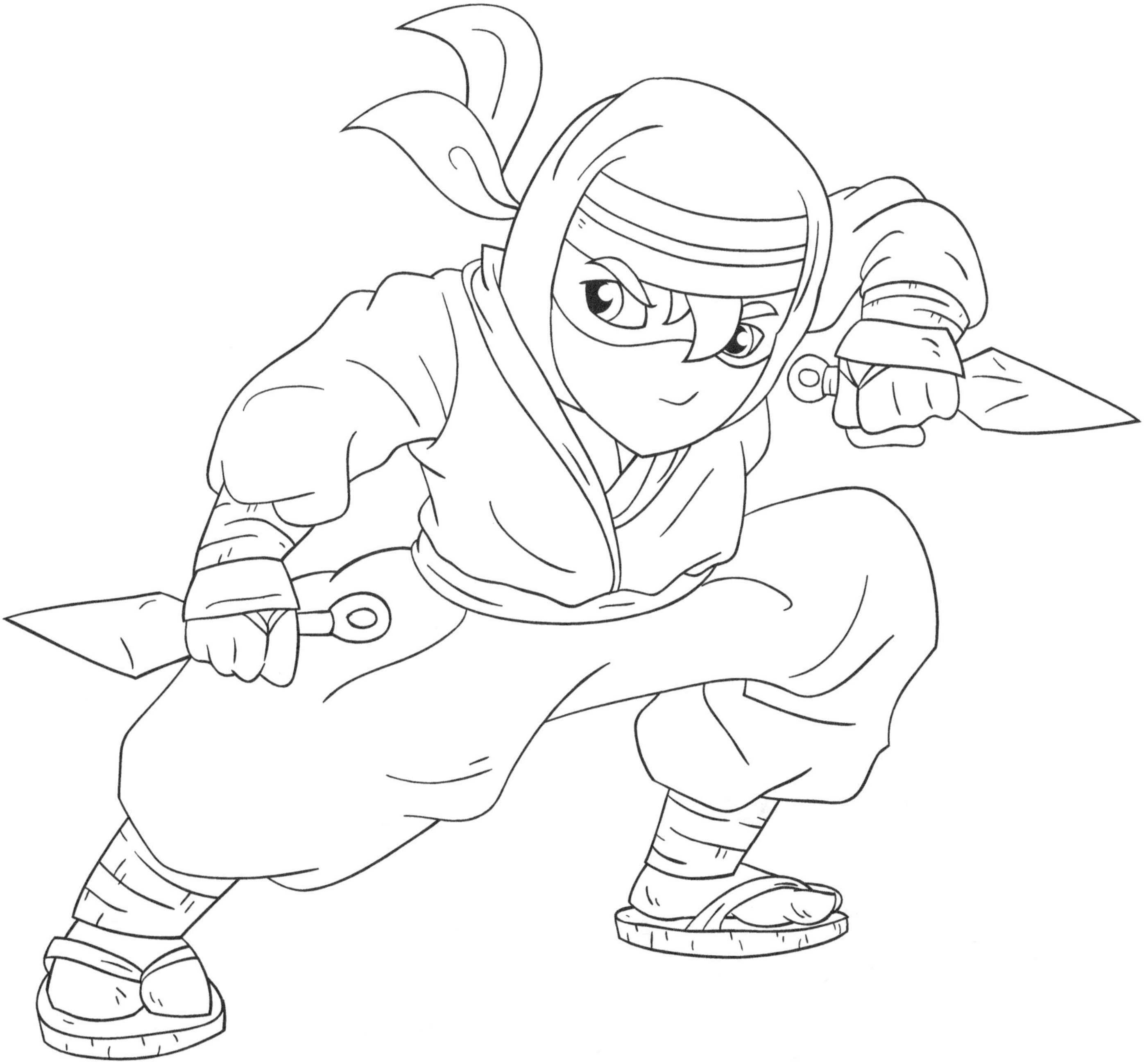

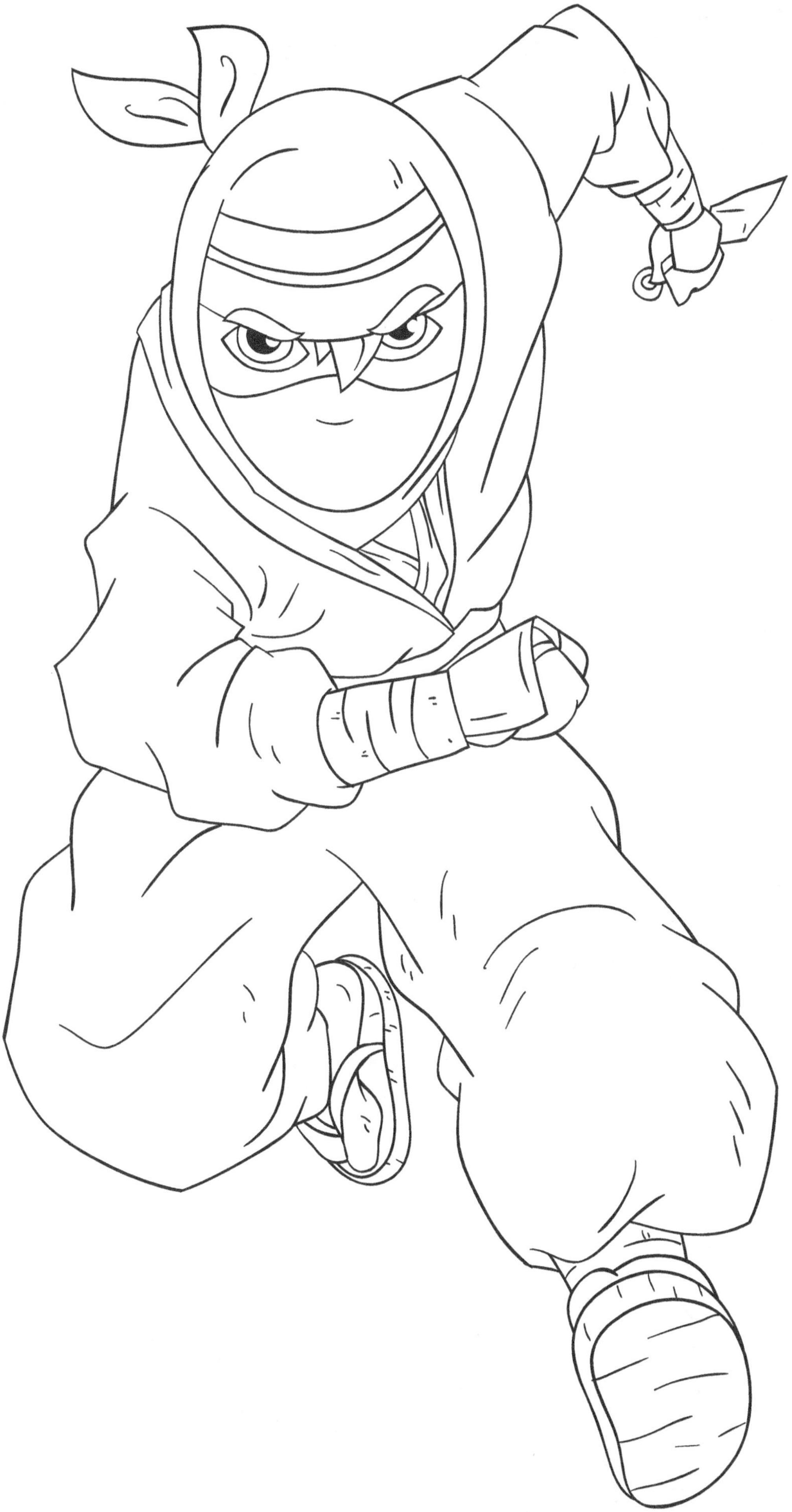

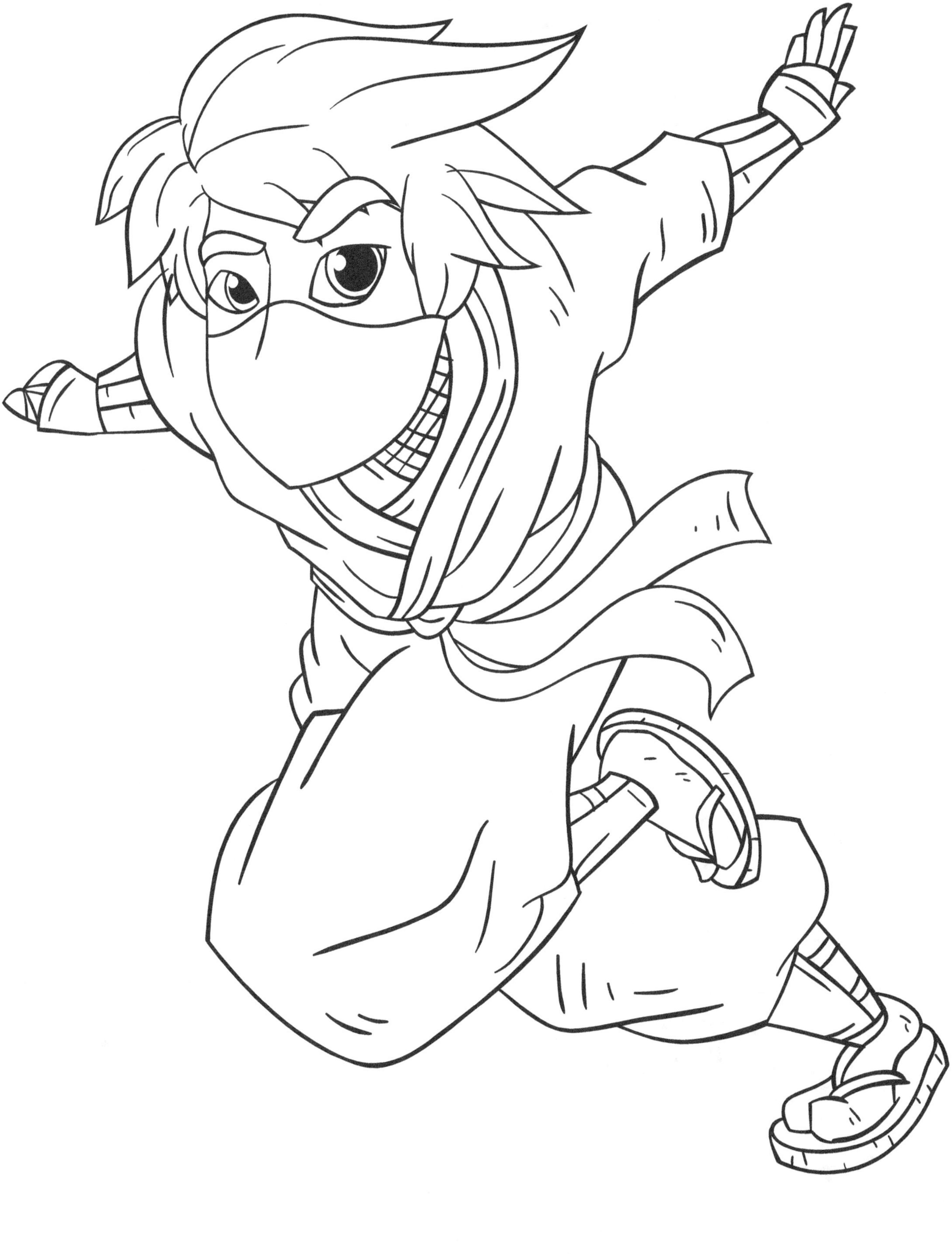

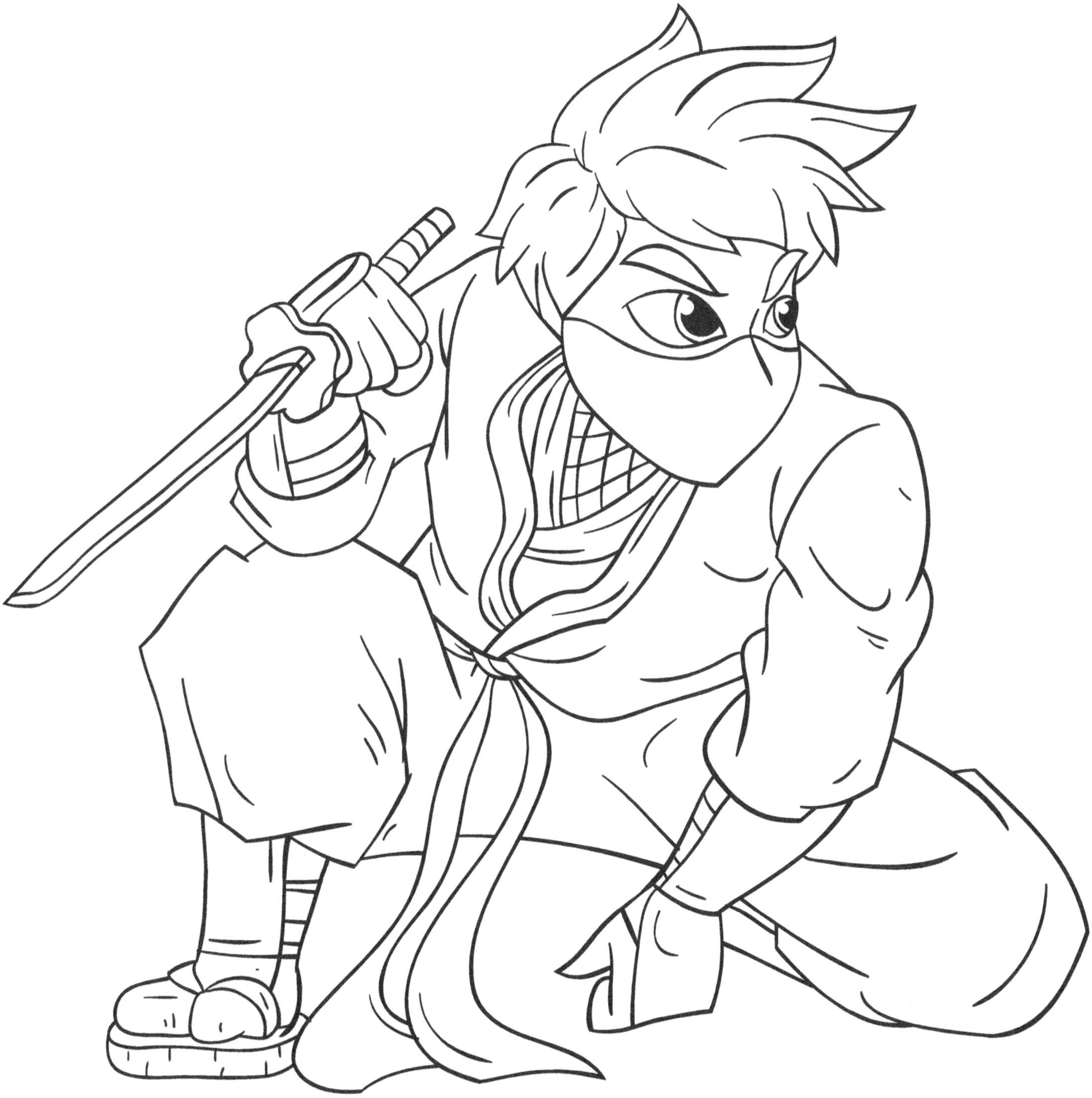

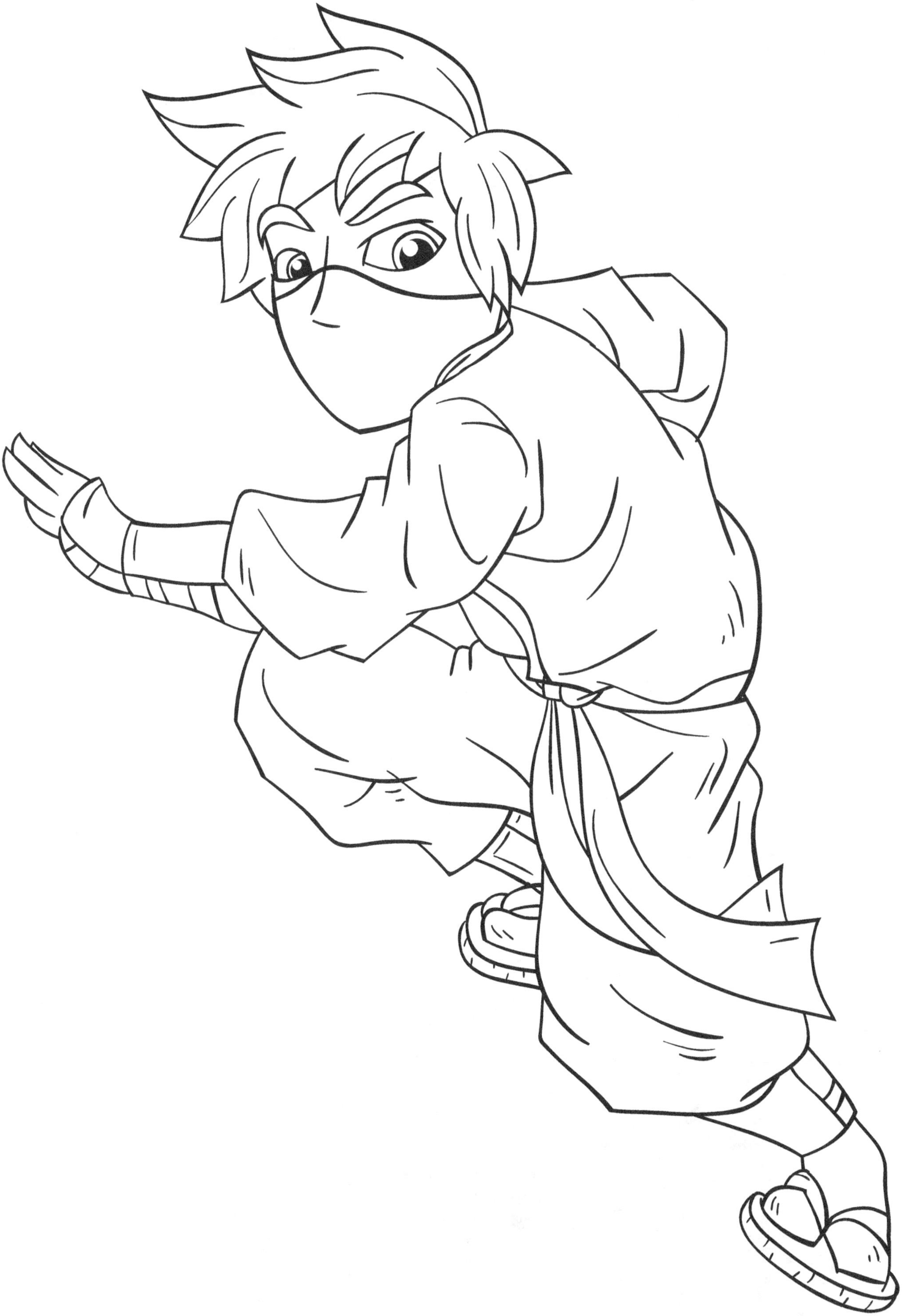

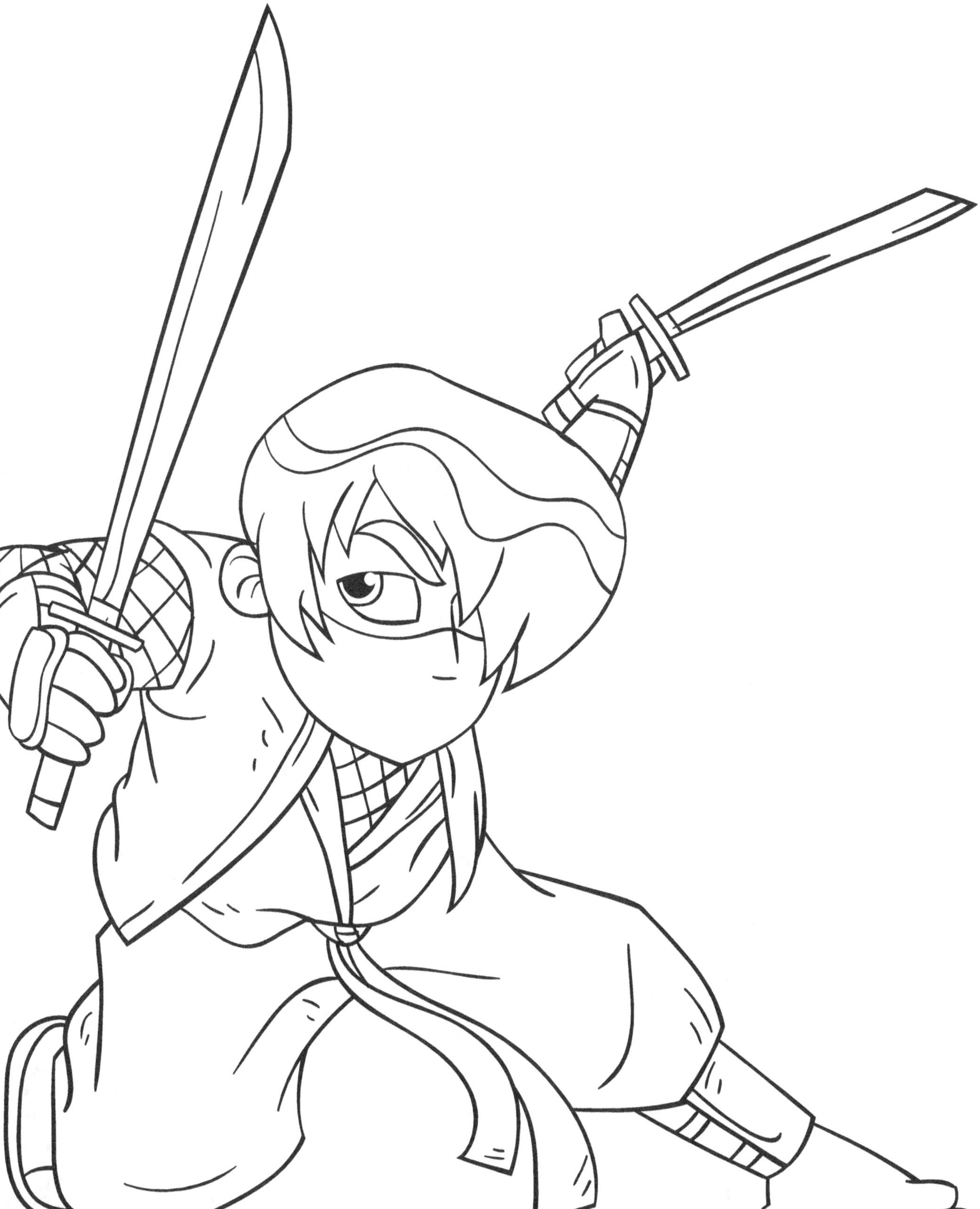

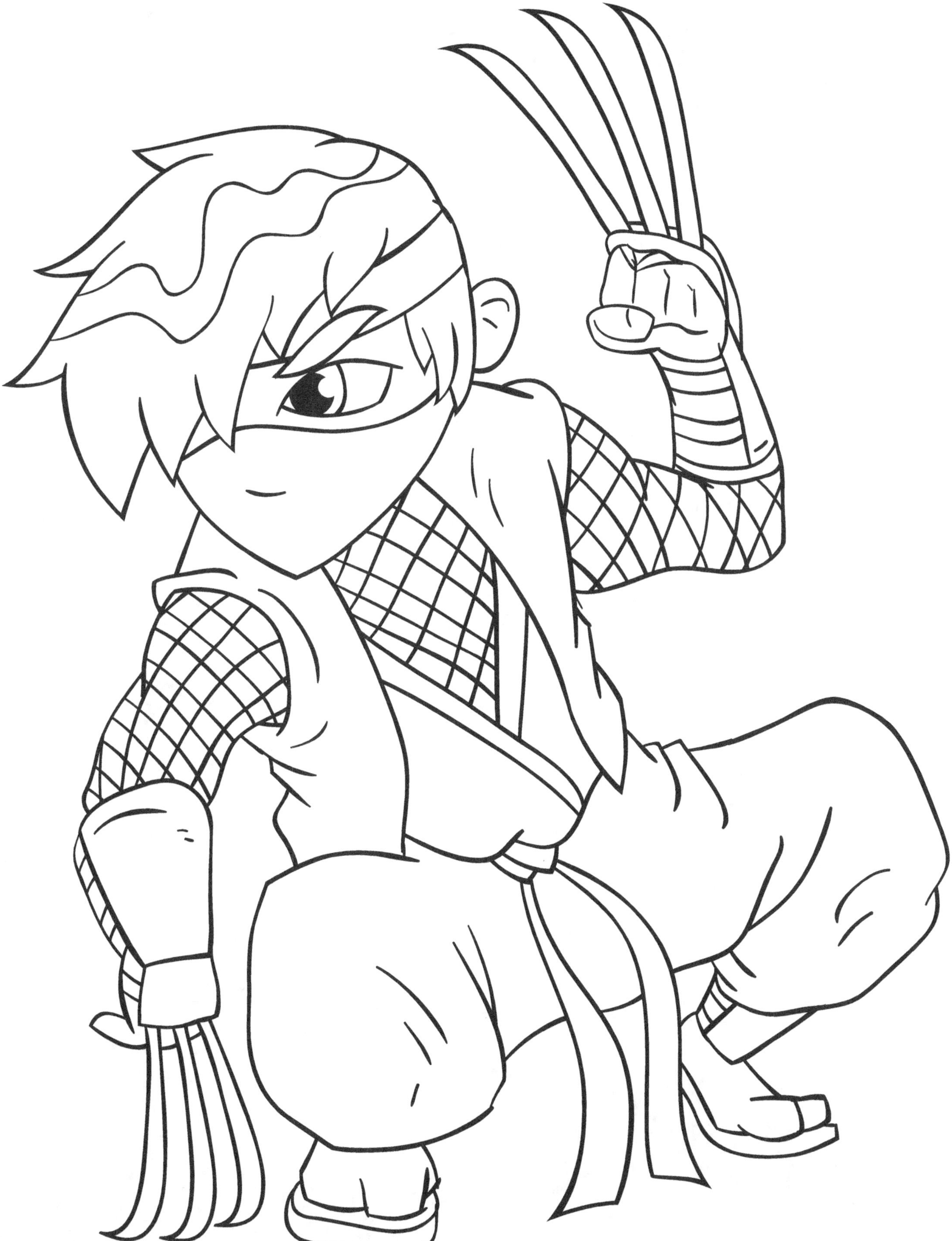

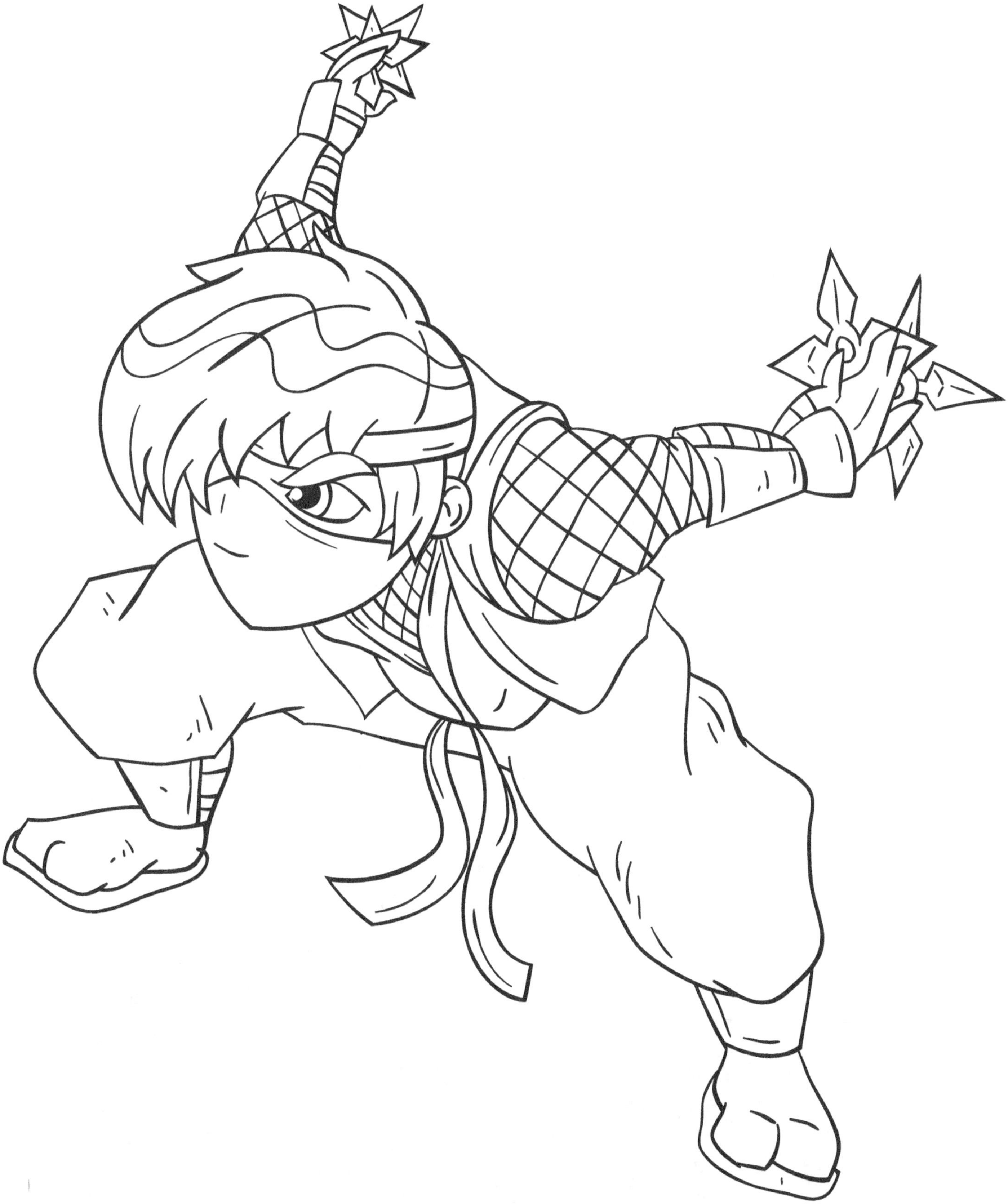

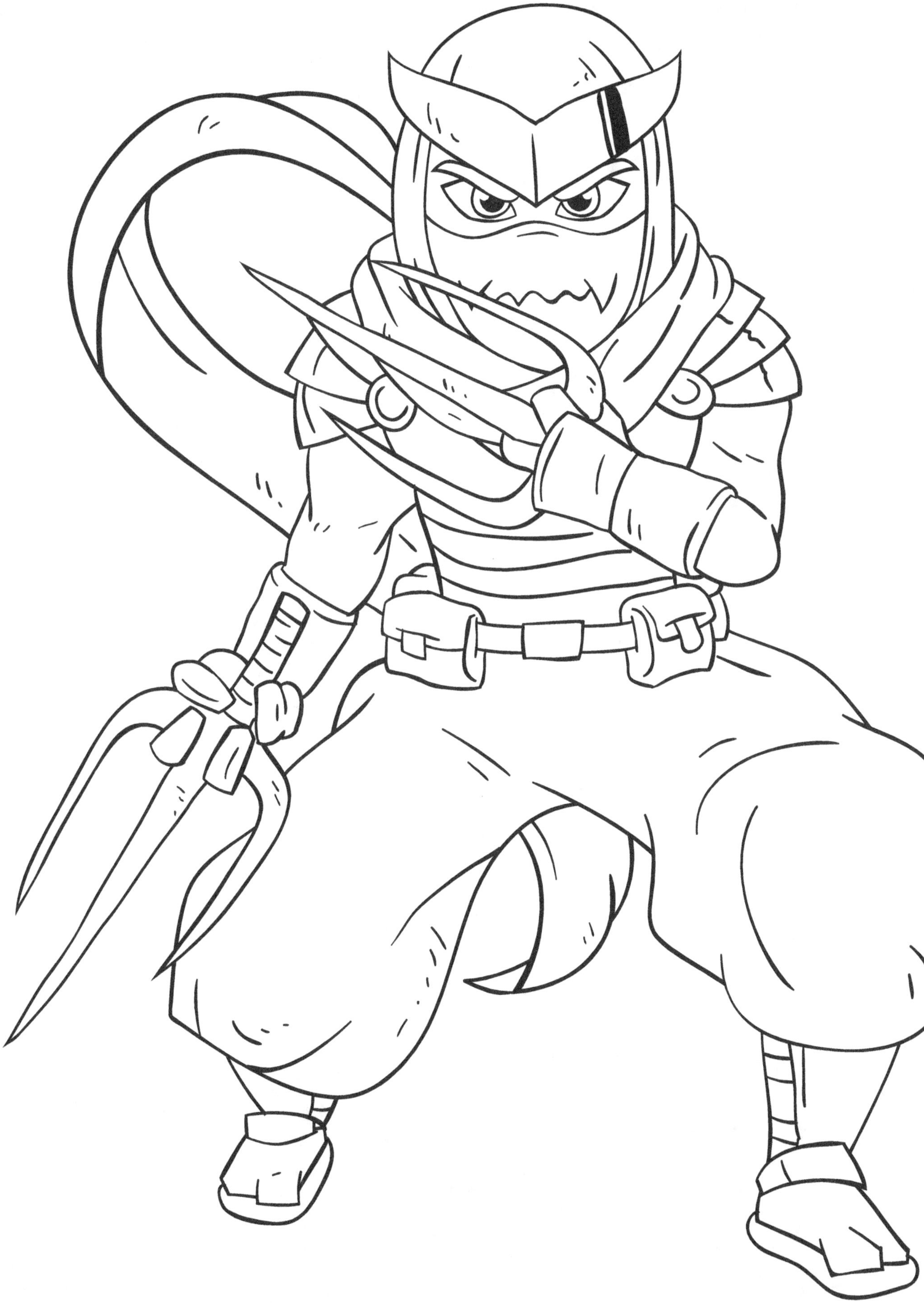

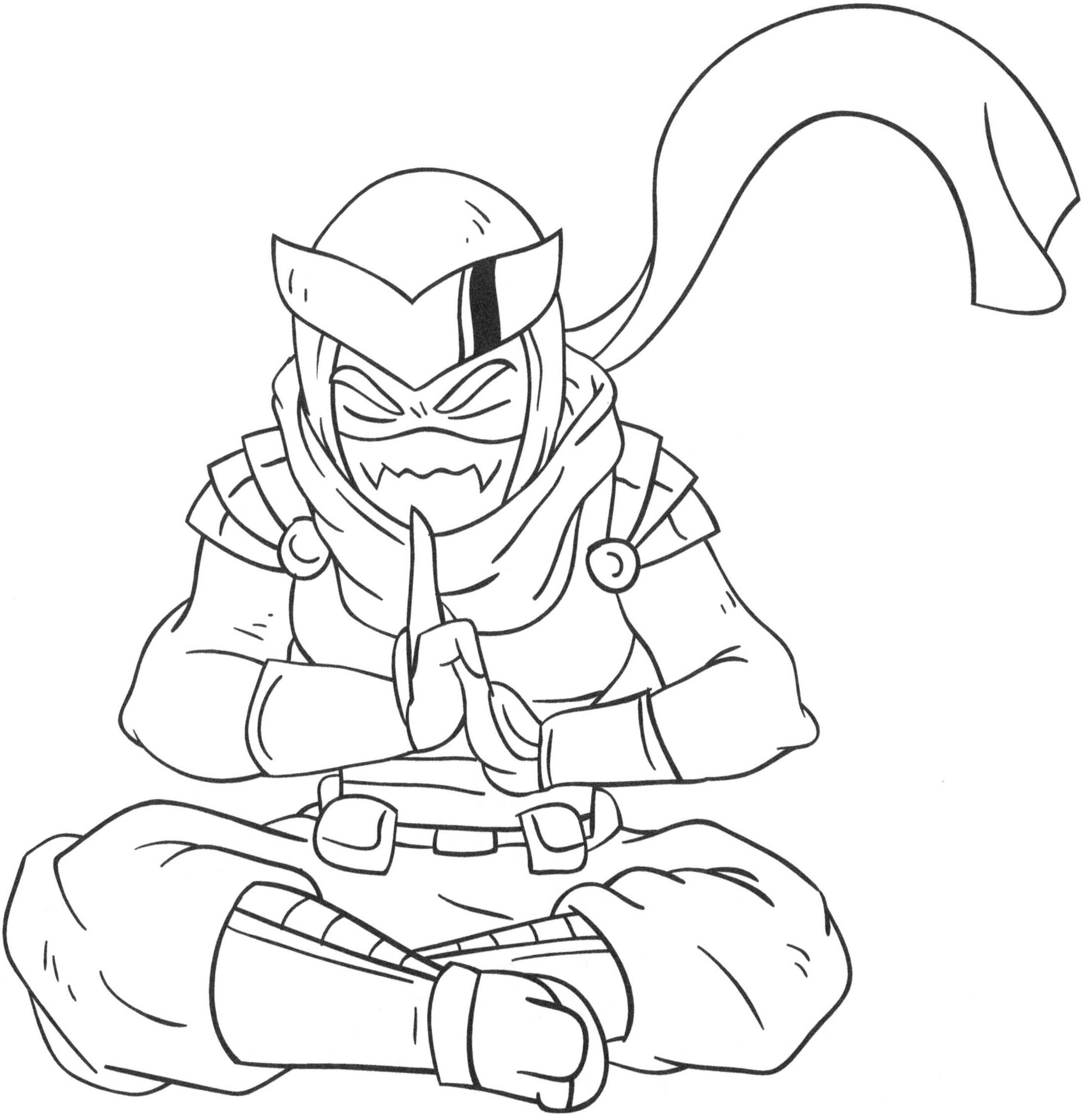

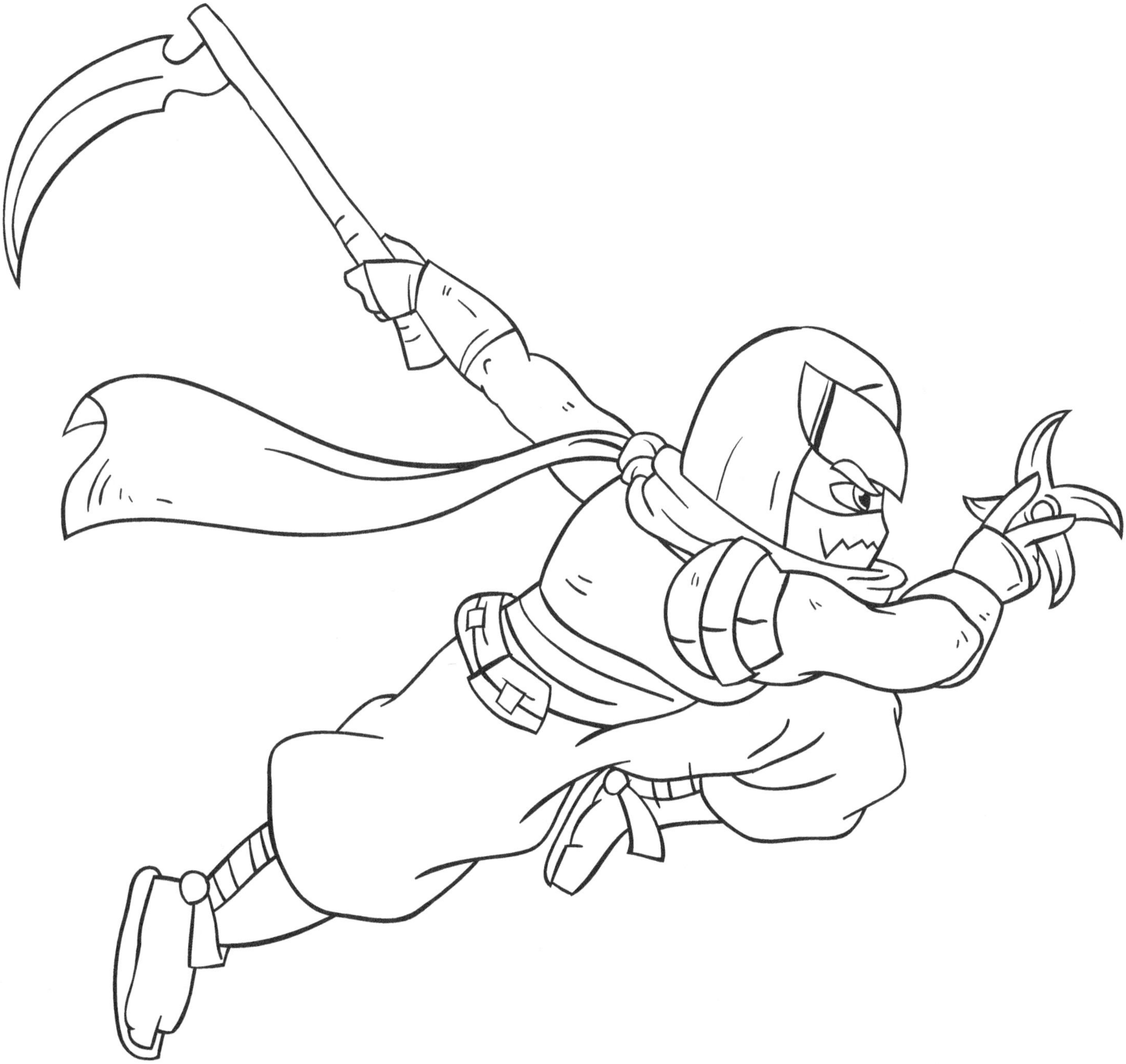

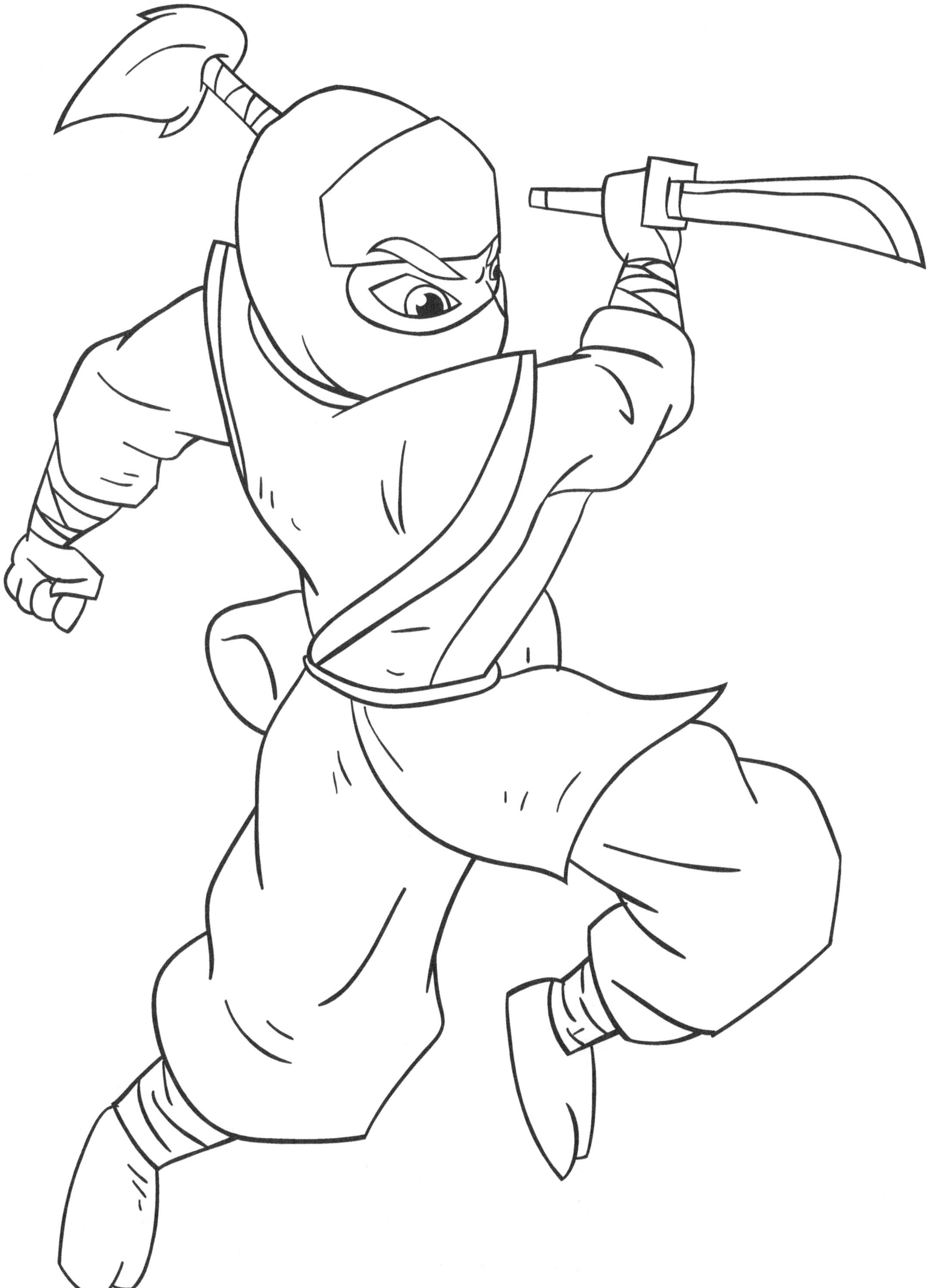

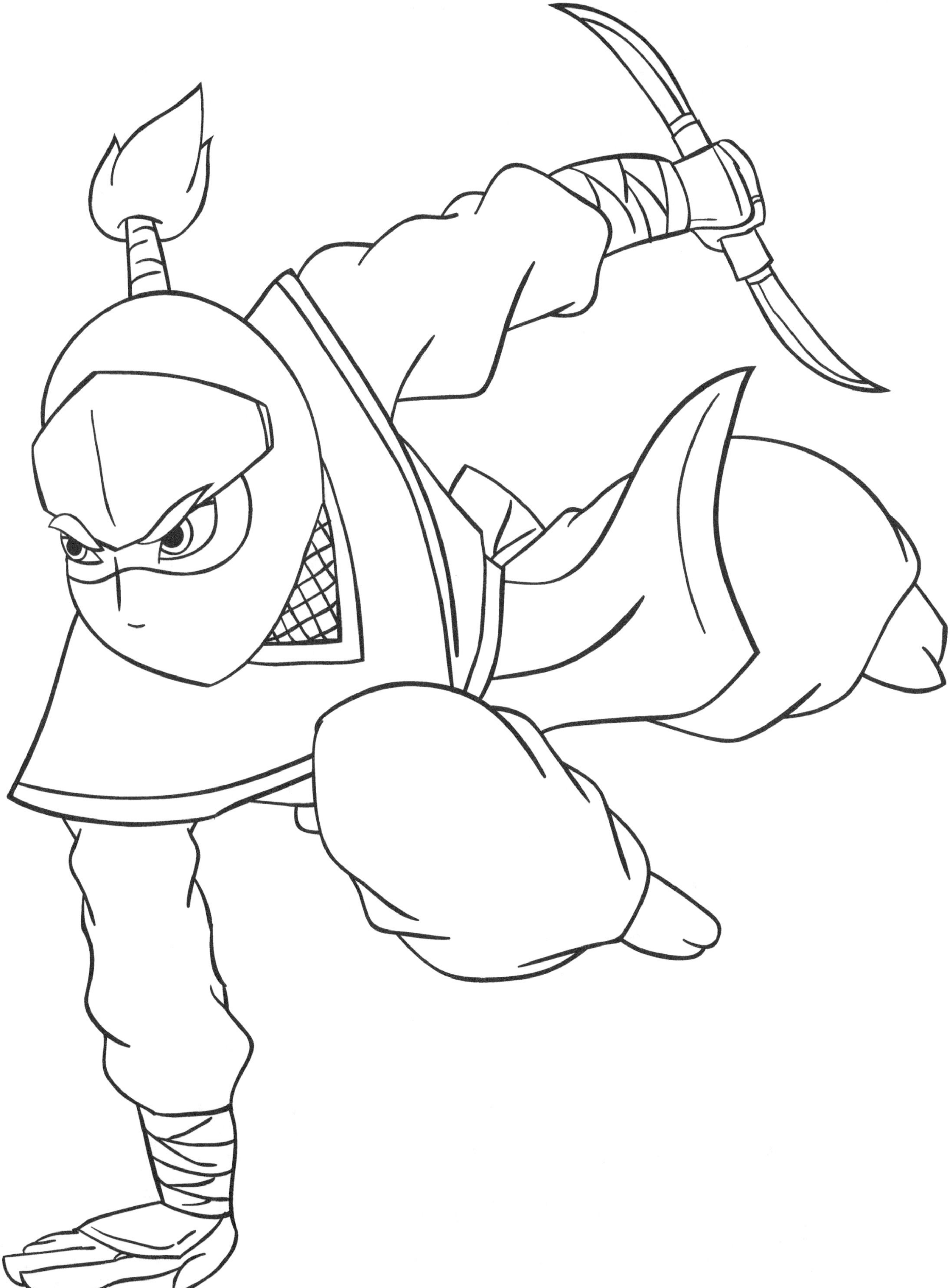

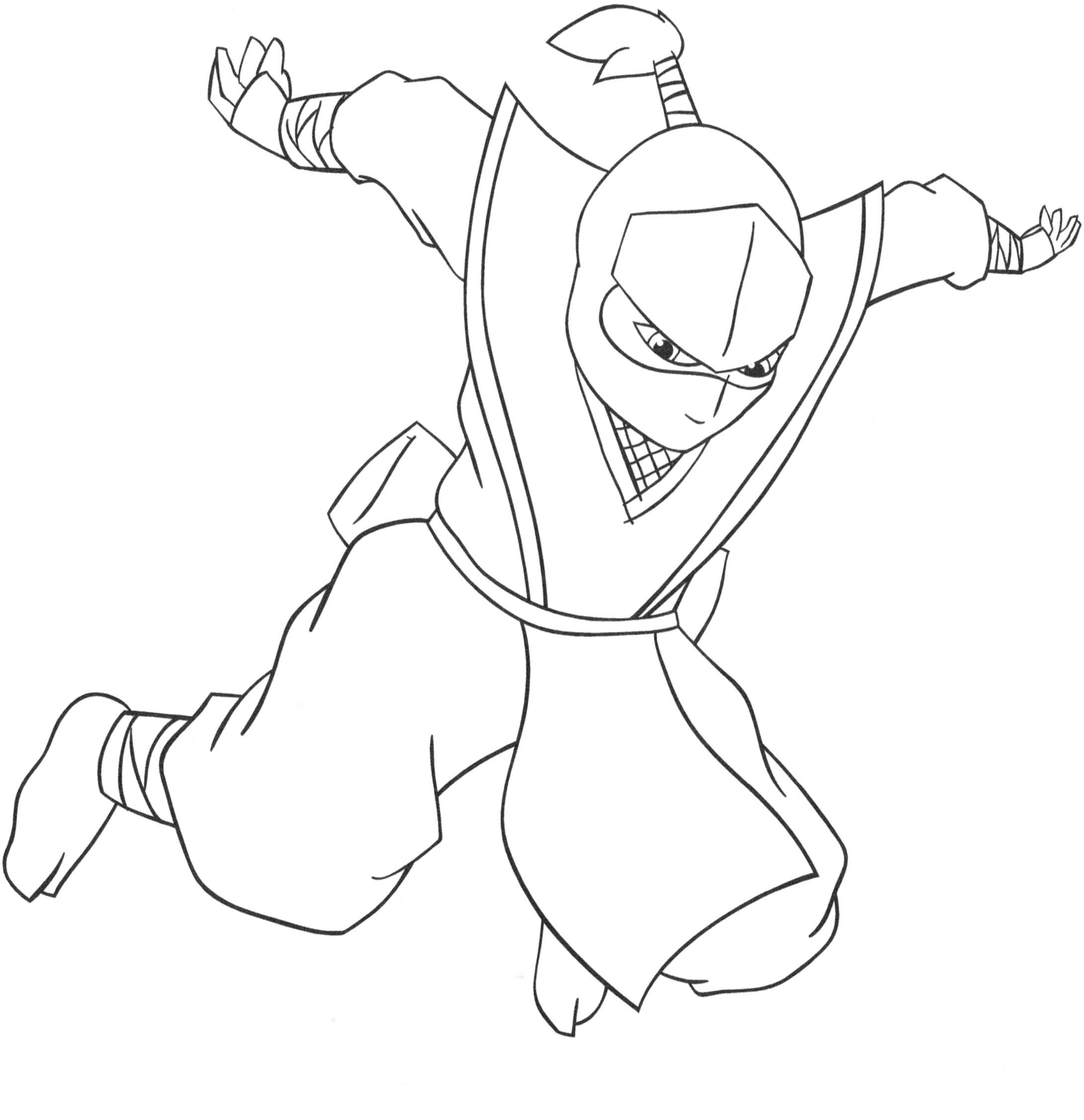

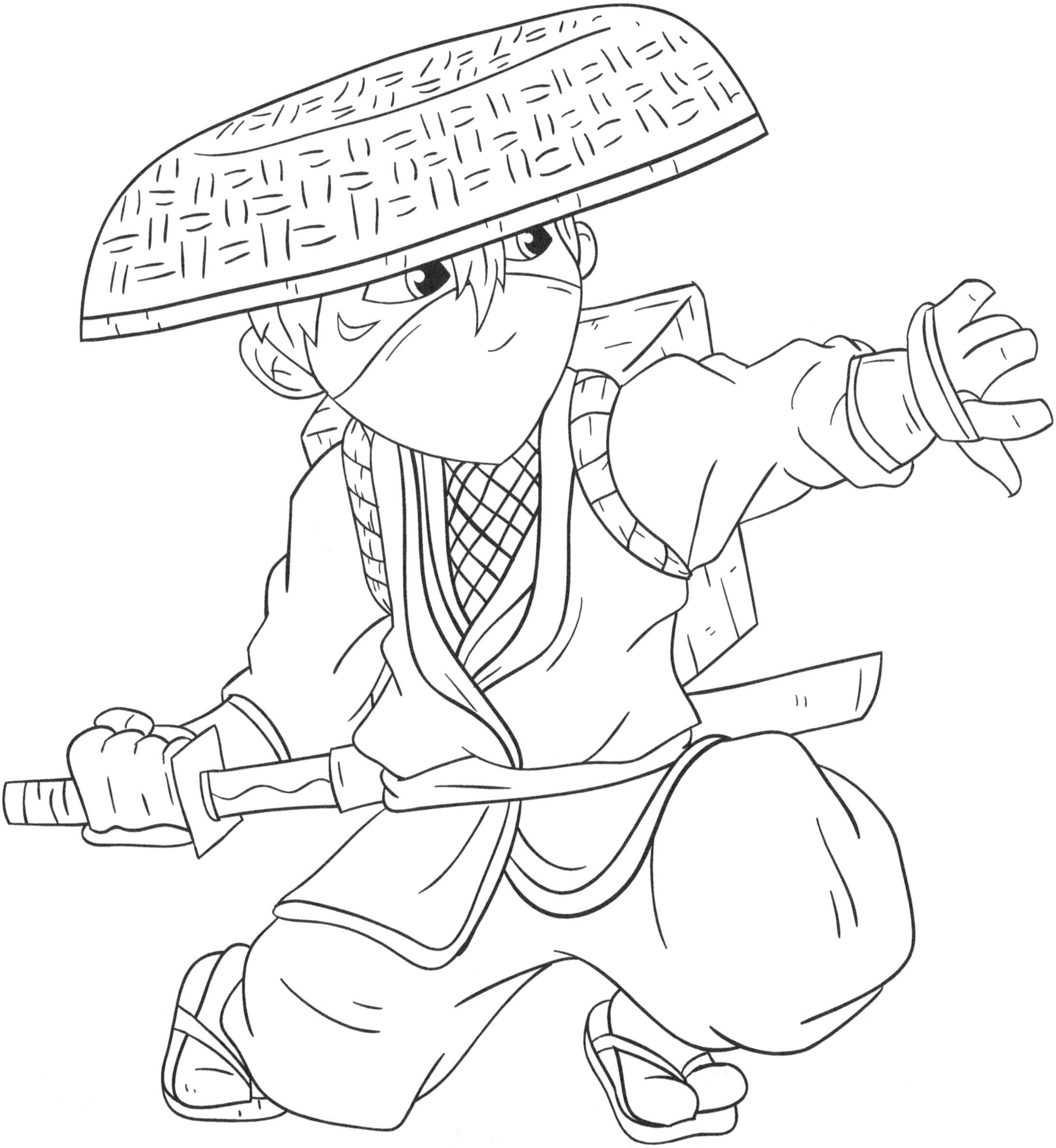

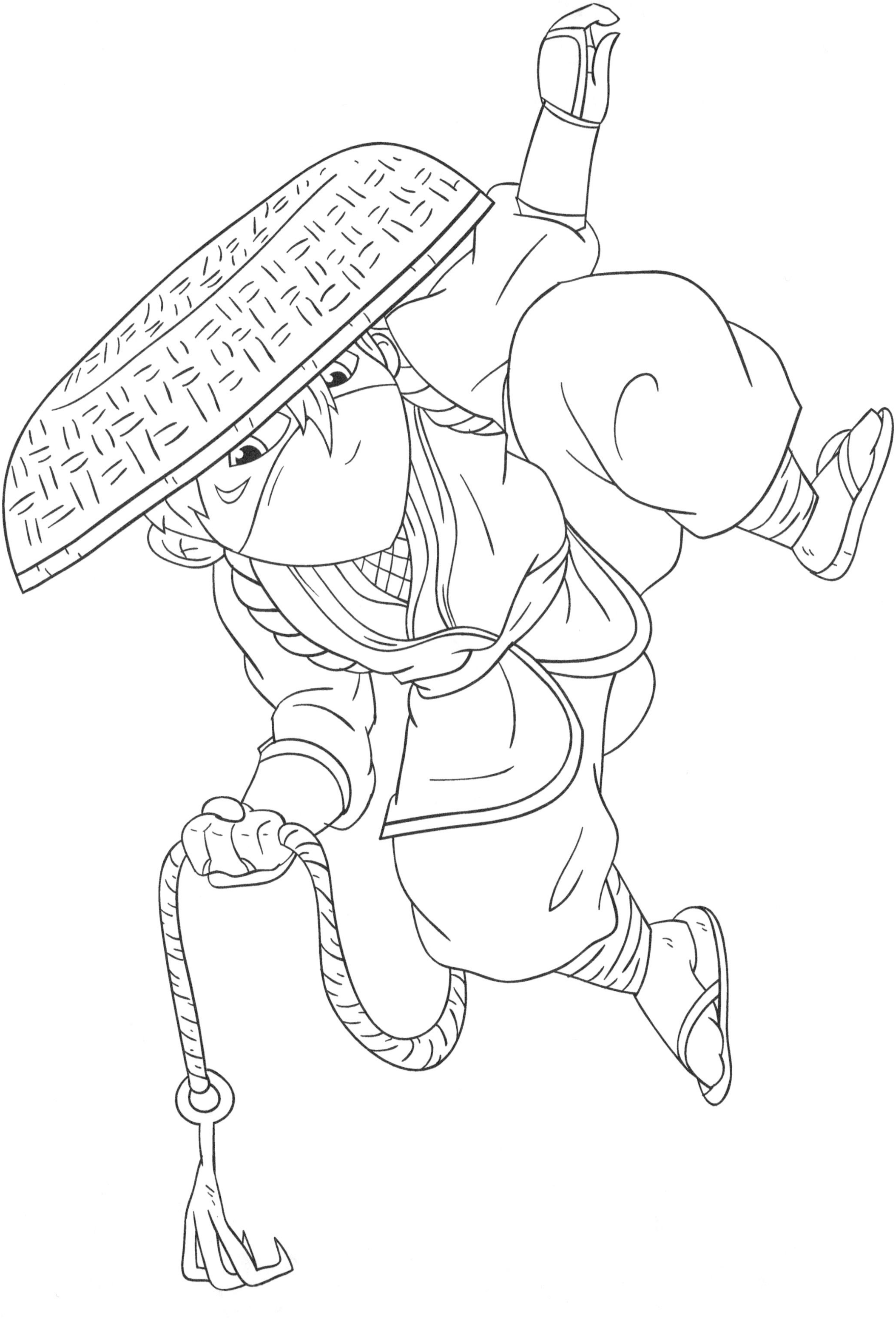

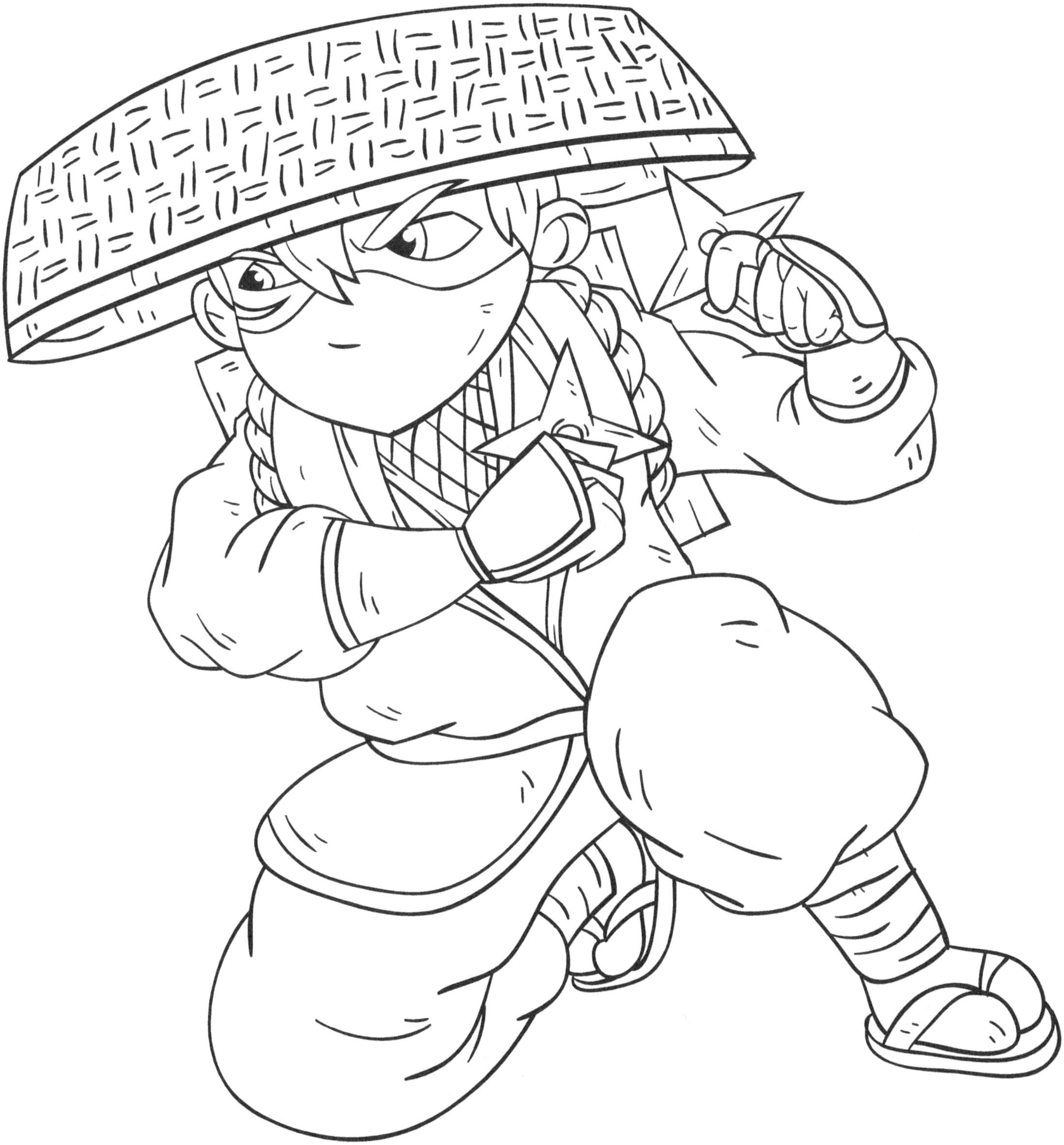

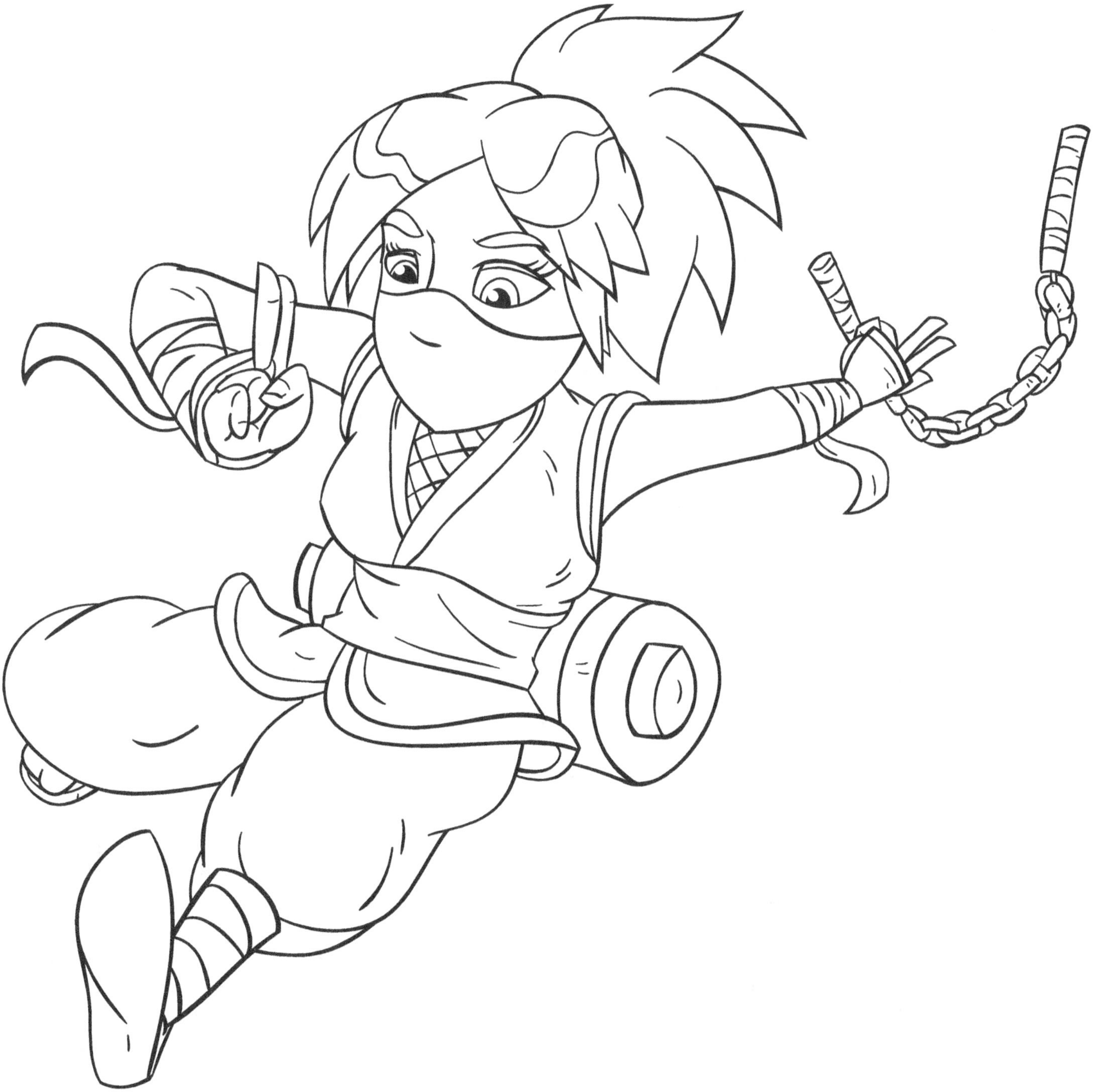

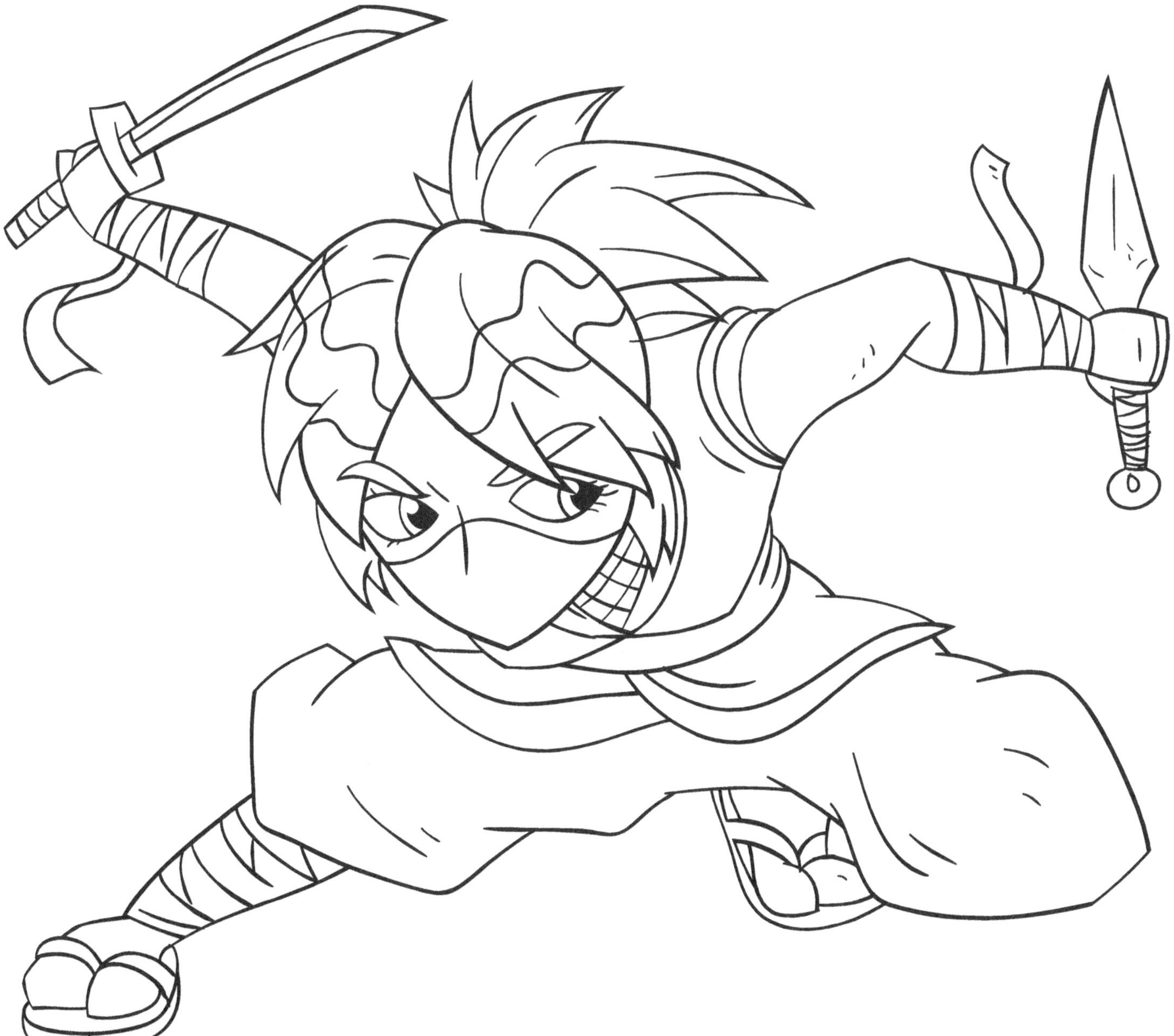

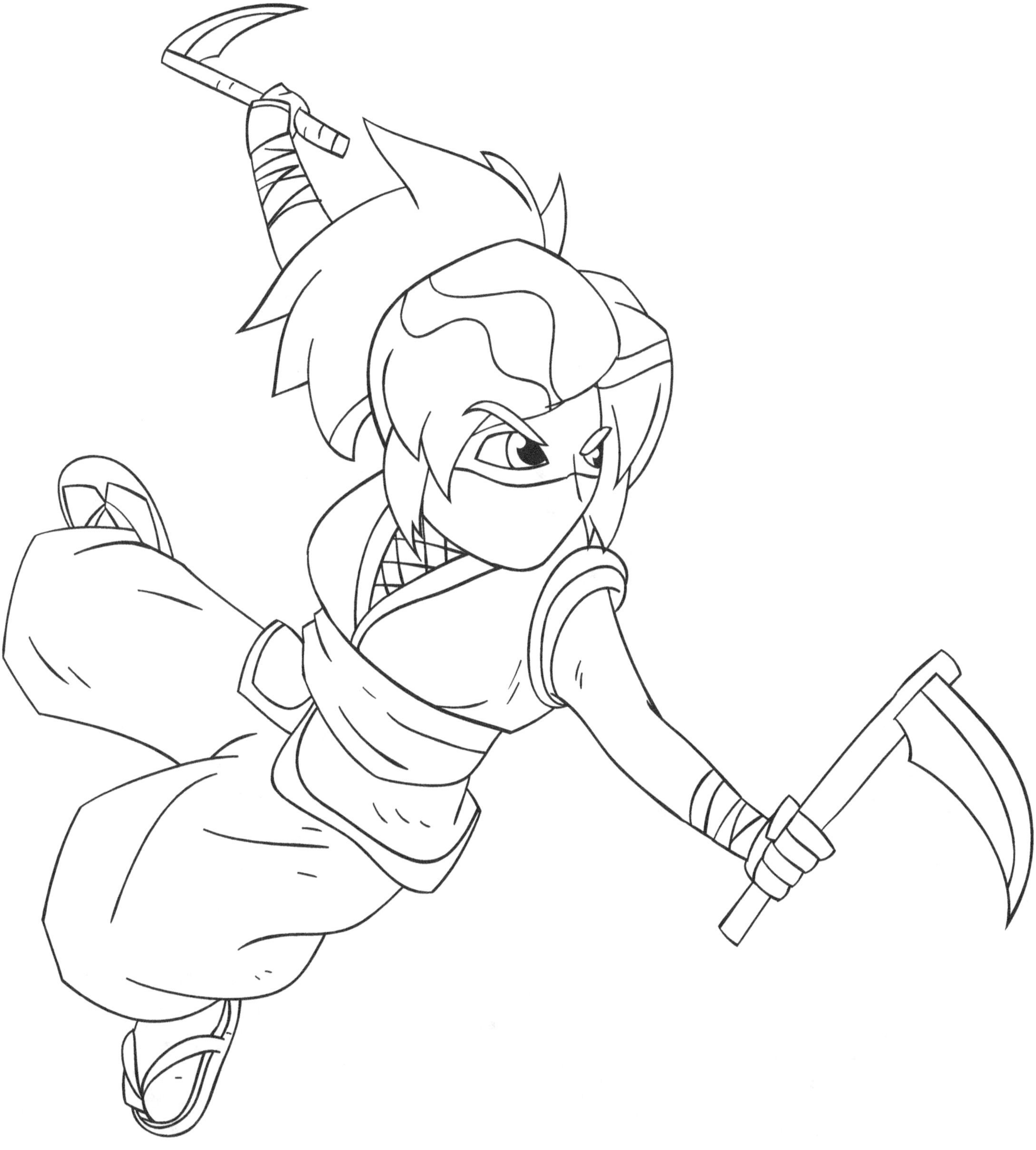

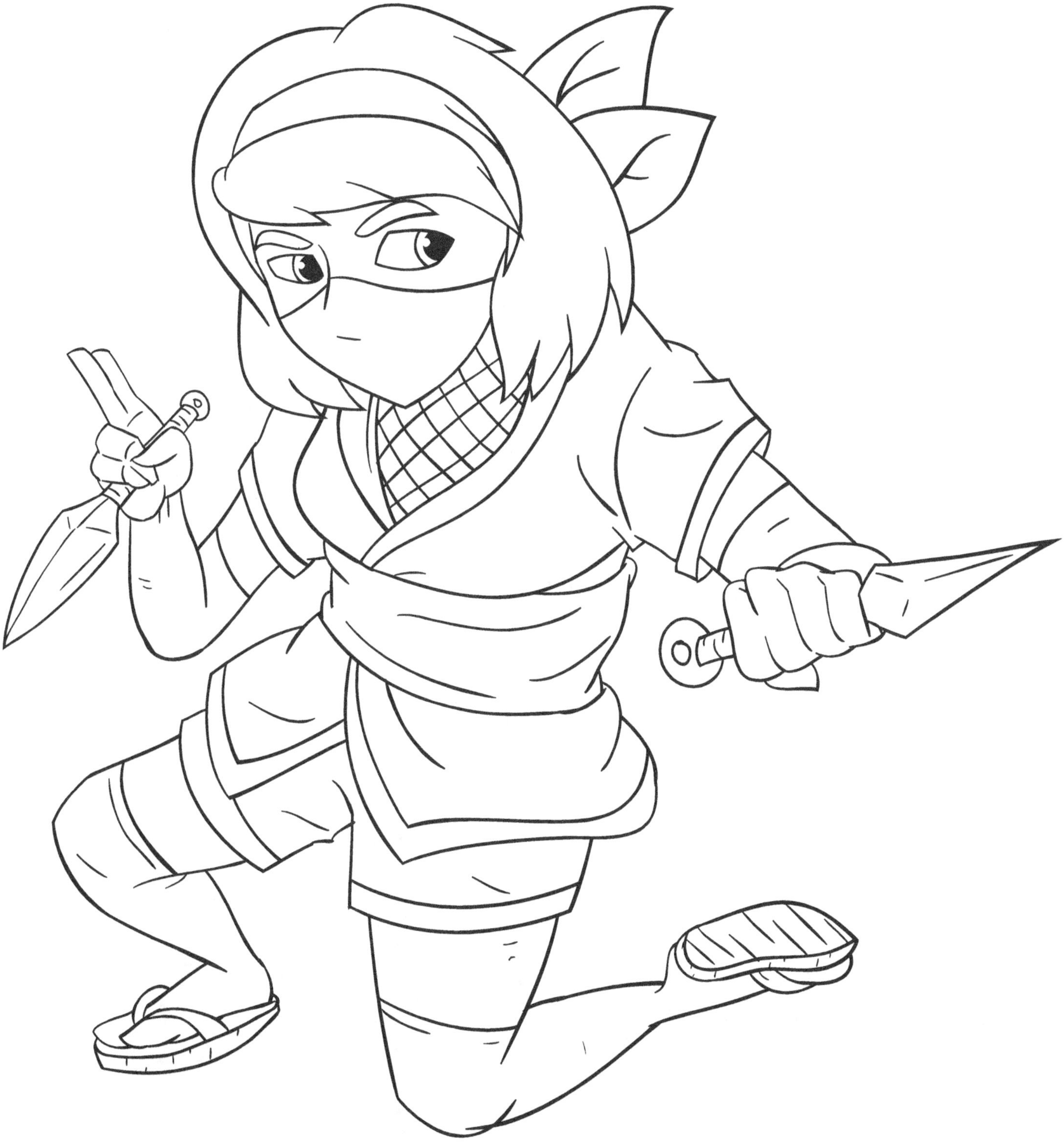

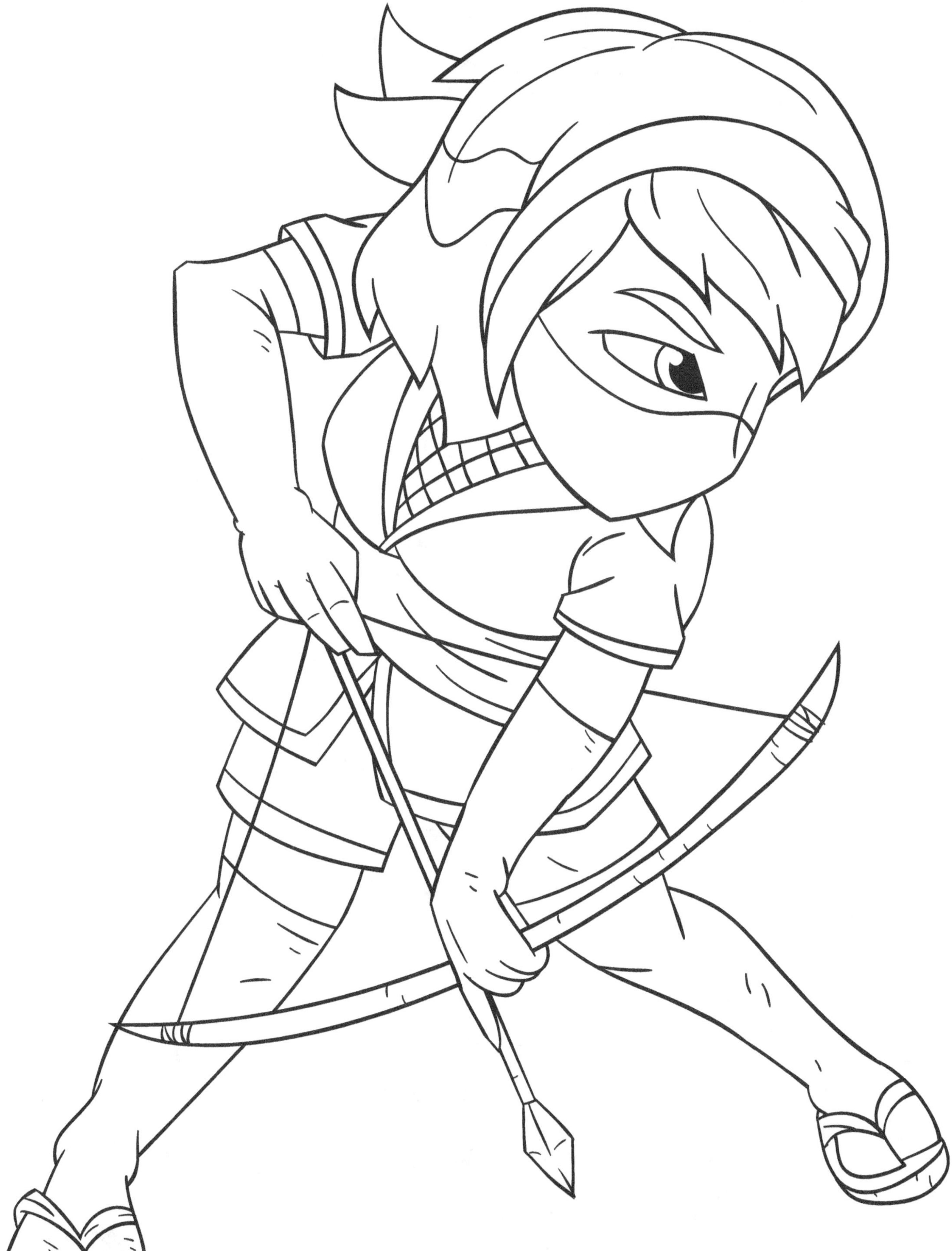

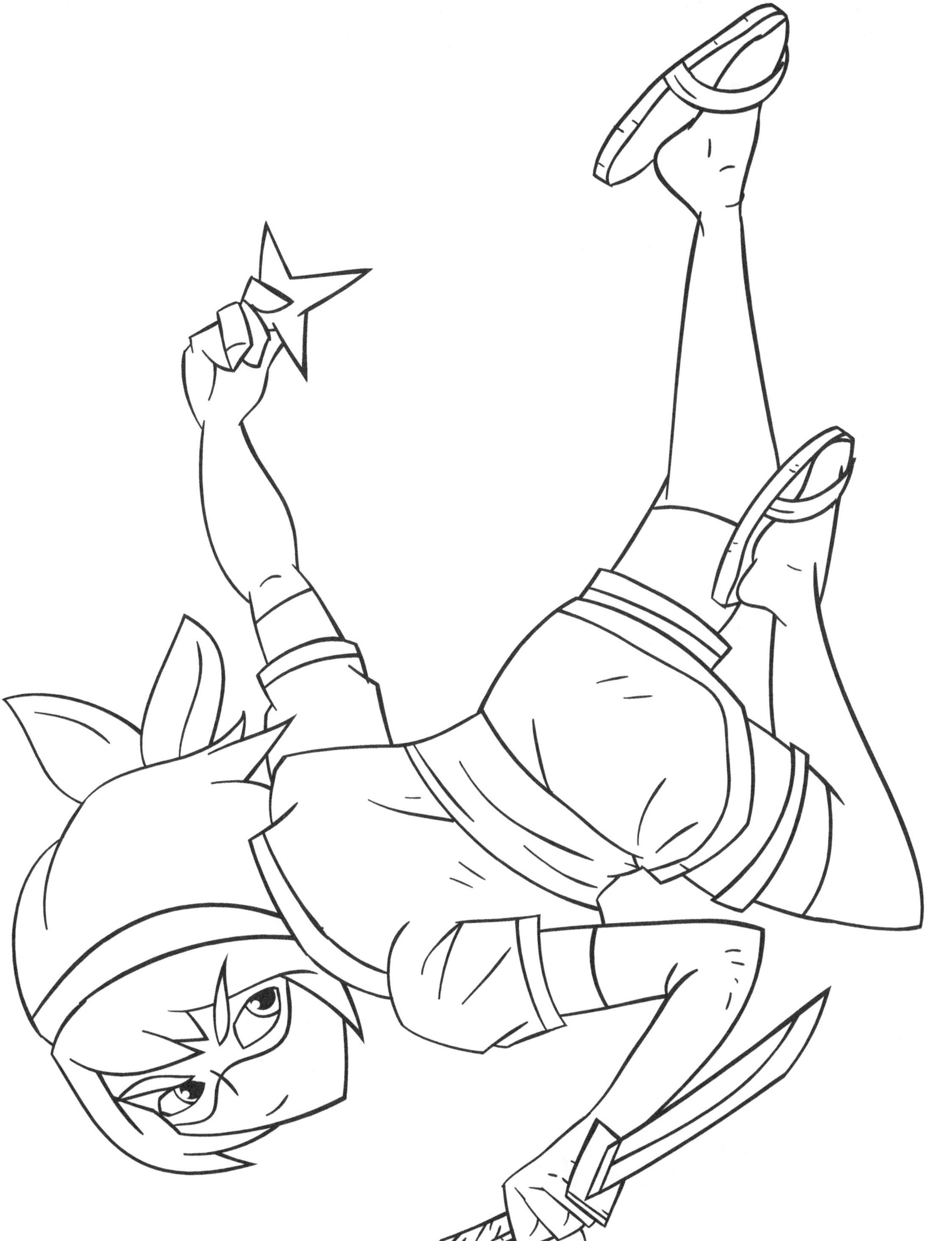